Punk Funk
© Beth Lenz 2005

Alfred's Rudimental Contest Solos

for the Intermediate Snare Drummer

Jay Wanamaker

Jay Wanamaker is highly regarded as a percussion educator, arranger and clinician. He holds a B.M.E. degree from the Crane School of Music at Potsdam State University in New York and an M.M. degree in Percussion Performance from the University of Kansas. Jay has instructed many mass percussion sections for special events including the 1984 Summer Olympic Games, the rededication of the Statue of Liberty, the Pan American Games, Super Bowl XXII and the McDonald's All-American High School Band. He has served on the music faculty at the University of Southern California and has authored over 50 percussion publications.

Jay is currently on the Board of Directors of the Percussive Arts Society and serves as General Manager for the Yamaha Corporation of America in Buena Park, California.

Dedicated to my daughter, Julie Ann Wanamaker

CONTENTS

Book production
and music engraving:
Bruce Goldes

Struttin'

Jay Wanamaker

Legend:

B.S. (Back Stick)	Strike the drumhead with the butt ends of the drumsticks.
R.S. (Rim Shot)	Strike the drum so that the stick strikes the drumhead and rim simultaneously.
T.S. (Tap Stick)	Click the shoulder of the right stick against the left stick (R), and then click the shoulder of the left stick against the right stick (L).
D.R.S. (Double Rim Shot)	Both sticks should strike the drum and rim simultaneously.
R.C. (Rim Click)	The butt end of the left stick strikes the rim while the left palm holds the shoulder of the stick in the center of the drumhead.

Funkster

Jay Wanamaker

Legend:

R.S. (Rim Shot)   Strike the drum so that the stick strikes the drumhead and rim simultaneously.

On-Line

Jay Wanamaker

Legend:

T.S. (Tap Stick)   Click the shoulder of the right stick against the left stick (R), and then click the shoulder of the left stick against the right stick (L).

Conquistador

Jay Wanamaker

Legend:

R.S. (Rim Shot)   Strike the drum so that the stick strikes the drumhead and rim simultaneously.

Chops Are Us

Jay Wanamaker

11

Legend:

R.S. (Rim Shot)   Strike the drum so that the stick strikes the drumhead and rim simultaneously.

S.S. (Stick Shot)   Strike the right stick on the left stick while the left stick is partway on the drum and rim.

B.S. (Back Stick)   Strike the drumhead with the butt ends of the drum sticks.

Free Flight

Jay Wanamaker

Legend:

R.S. (Rim Shot)   Strike the drum so that the stick strikes the drumhead and rim simultaneously.

S.S. (Stick Shot)   Strike the right stick on the left stick while the left stick is partway on the drum and rim.

T.S. (Tap Stick)   Click the shoulder of the right stick against the left stick (R), and then click the shoulder of the left stick against the right stick (L).

14

Cyclone

Jay Wanamaker

15

Legend:

R.S. (Rim Shot)   Strike the drum so that the stick strikes the drumhead and rim simultaneously.

Chop Builders

Jay Wanamaker